# THE ART OF GOOD GOVERNANCE

*Seven rules for growth and stability*

**Dictum Press, Oxford, UK**
*dictumpress.com*

An abbreviated version of this booklet appears as Appendix 2 in *The Leadership Files: From around the world, across a century* by Vaughan Roberts, Ajith Fernando, John Stott *et al*. Foreword by Joni Eareckson-Tada. (Oxford, Dictum 2020. ISBN 978-1-8380972-0-2)

This edition, 2025

ISBN 978-1-915934-26-0
EPub ISBN 978-1-915934-25-3

All rights reserved.

© Dictum Press
© Foreword: Charles Clayton

Cover design by David Powell
Page design by Chris Gander

# THE ART OF GOOD GOVERNANCE

*Seven rules for growth and stability*

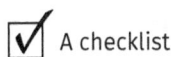

A checklist

*This short book has been compiled by Julia Cameron of Dictum Press, in consultation with senior leaders and board members of national and international ministries.*

*Dictum is grateful to Charles Clayton for the Foreword, and to the CEOs and board chairs who commented on sections as the 'seven rules' were being completed.*

# CONTENTS

| | |
|---|---|
| Foreword by Charles Clayton | 9 |
| Introduction | 10 |
| **Seven rules of good governance** | 14 |
| 1. Role and purpose of an effective board<br>    *Principles, policy, and practice* | 17 |
| 2. Profile of an effective board<br>    *Facets of wisdom and experience* | 19 |
| 3. Orientation of new board members | 26 |
| 4. Guarding theological/financial integrity<br>    *Theological integrity*<br>    *Financial integrity* | 27 |
| 5. The CEO's role in relation to the ministry and to the board<br>    *Reporting and appraisal of the CEO*<br>    *Appointment of a new CEO* | 31 |
| 6. Board protocol<br>    *Handling major issues*<br>    *Cycle of business*<br>    *Conflicts of interest*<br>    *Dependent committees* | 38 |
| 7. Supporting the board | 40 |
| **To conclude** | 42 |

# FOREWORD

This little gem is full of seasoned wisdom, making it a useful resource for anyone interested in the governance of Christian organizations.

It is *brief*, but hints at wider resources and selects the essential actions drawn from the collective experience of many others before us.

It is *sane*, providing straightforward and realistic ways to develop good governance, avoiding lofty dogma or unrealistic ideals.

It is *practical*, giving a check list of things to do right away, while hinting at the important underlying principles. This is a great way to get on with the job without delay, and build up your understanding as you go on.

In governance we are entrusted with something valuable on behalf of others, so let's do a really good job in it. The Apostle Paul said, 'Now it is required that those who have been given a trust must prove faithful.' (1 Corinthians 4:2, NIV)

Charles Clayton
*oxfordleaders.com*

# INTRODUCTION

Welcome to the seven rules of governance. They are intended to be liberating rules, as once these stakes are firmly in the ground, boards have the freedom to focus on the ministry itself, knowing that the structure and governance is secure.

This material is available as a short book so that each member of the board can have a copy. It is hoped that it will provide a simple guide to new board members, and enable all members, new and long-standing, to keep the board aligned to its purpose, enabling it to run along well-oiled tracks. There is no eighth rule, but you can't get by on six.

Recent years have seen tragic closures, or takeovers, of charities, ministries, and publishing houses.[1] Some closed for financial reasons, a few were mired in scandal, and others lost their way. Behind each is a story, and some stories began several years or even decades before the closure, takeover, or scandal. Difficulties, even tragedies, were just waiting to happen. The seed of the problem may have lain in its structures – perhaps through decisions taken without foresight. Or perhaps there were inadequate

---

1. The terms 'ministry', 'mission' and 'movement' are used interchangeably throughout. Boards and CEOs of confessional publishing houses which operate as businesses will also identify with these terms. Both theological integrity and financial integrity are core to such boards.

safeguards in place for accountability between the board and the CEO, or between the CEO and senior management.[2] Or the problem may have been in weak management; or in over-dependence on a particular income stream; or in lack of forward planning. In whatever way it came about, board members showed negligence in not asking (or perhaps not seeing) the critical questions which needed to be asked. Decisions made, both in the present and in the past, can carry hidden costs for the future.

> *DECISIONS CAN CARRY HIDDEN COSTS FOR THE FUTURE*

The responsibility for the health of any organization always lies finally with its Trustees. This is why board membership is critical to get right: those who have the ministry at heart, who have good spiritual judgment, and the skills and experience to lead.

Furthermore, it is vital for the board to appoint members who will have time to prepare for meetings. Discussion will be the poorer and mistakes in direction can happen unintentionally when papers are read in a rush before the meeting, or not read at all.

---

2. Accountability for Christian leaders of organizations must always be seen in two ways: formal and informal. Here we consider formal accountability relationships – although we also comment briefly on the importance of informal structures.

**THE ART OF GOOD GOVERNANCE**

We haven't engaged with the use of online meetings, which will be for discussion in your own context. A virtual meeting could serve a focused discussion for a sub-committee well. But for the full board, it is worth weighing the benefits of having half, or two-thirds, of the meetings in person for everyone, as the relational aspect of board life is vital to its working together. We touch on this later.

> *THE RELATIONAL ASPECT OF BOARD LIFE IS VITAL*

The principles presented here are equally applicable to boards and senior staff of schools; to church leaders; and to any charity or movement with a governing body.

◆ ◆ ◆

# SEVEN RULES OF
GOOD GOVERNANCE

# SEVEN RULES OF GOOD GOVERNANCE

A Christian mission founded in the UK celebrated its 150th anniversary a few years ago. At the anniversary event, the senior team sang a spoof version of the classic 1977 Bee Gees song 'Stayin' Alive', rewritten as 'Stayin' Aligned'. The mission's 150-year history bore testimony to the way, under God, it had stayed aligned to its original purpose and values.[3] To keep an organization aligned, board members need to imbibe its history and its values – a recurring refrain, as we shall see. The CEO must work to nurture an awareness of these in the staff team, interns, and volunteers. To stay aligned requires constant vigilance.

Members of a governing body are the Trustees[4] of that ministry and, as this name implies, they are entrusted with its life. They carry responsibility for passing the ministry on to the next generation, effective in its calling, and in a spiritually-healthy state. This is their responsibility and their joy.

---

3. OMF International, founded by James Hudson Taylor in 1865 as the China Inland Mission.

4. Some ministries or institutions may have a board and a separate body of Trustees. In these cases, the board is no less responsible for keeping the ministry aligned, so for simplicity, the term 'board' here refers to both levels of governance.

## SEVEN RULES

History has shown that good governance is vital to assure success in the outcomes of the work. Conversely, where governance is weak, the whole ministry will be weakened and its future effectiveness can be put at risk.

> *WHERE GOVERNANCE IS WEAK, THE WHOLE MINISTRY WILL BE WEAKENED*

An invitation to serve on a board is not to be taken lightly; nor indeed to be regarded as a means of conferring status. While carrying significant responsibility, it is, as the verb conveys, a way of serving.

We hope that what follows will be of help for those who serve as board members of mission agencies, seminaries, or Christian publishing houses. It is intended as a checklist, rather than a handbook.[5]

A Christian's *first* priority will naturally be his / her local church. Alongside the local church, it is not possible to serve more than one of two other ministries well. An invitation to join a board may need to be declined in order to serve more fully on other fronts. While there can be no hard-and-fast rule, some ministries will ask that board members place their ministry no lower down than third in terms of priority. For the board to function well between

---

[5]. The Charity Commission in your country will provide resources / publications outlining the duties of Trustees.

meetings, its members must be able to do more than be present each time it meets.

The seven rules assume that board members understand the legal requirements of charity Trustees as laid out by their government, and that they are conversant with the body's constitution or Memorandum and Articles. Confessional charities are assumed to have in place a doctrinal basis, to serve as the movement's anchor; and a clear document on vision and values.

The doctrinal basis may be borrowed from another ministry. For example, many evangelical movements have adopted the doctrinal basis of the IFES movement in their country, or the 2010 Cape Town Confession of Faith. For all Christian traditions, the doctrinal basis should be seen as a 'minimum' and a 'maximum'. That is, board members should gladly adhere to each part. If a person wants to add an additional clause, he or she is requiring more than the ministry requires.

> *THE DOCTRINAL BASIS SHOULD BE SEEN AS A 'MINIMUM' AND A 'MAXIMUM'*

And so we come to our 'seven rules'.

# 1
# ROLE AND PURPOSE OF AN EFFECTIVE BOARD
☑

The board ensures the vision and strategic direction of the organization / ministry. It oversees the ministry through the CEO, who in turn works with his / her senior team. The board is responsible for:

(a) the ministry's continuing strategic alignment with its purpose and values, as it moves forward;

(b) its ongoing financial viability and financial good conduct;

(c) its theological integrity;

(d) its statutory compliance (such as annual reports to the Charity Commission, Companies House or other regulators); and ensuring both policies and working protocols are in place for people's legal protection, eg with regard to employment law, safeguarding, cyber security.

It is important to distinguish between 'governance' (the role of the board) and 'management' (delegated by the board to the CEO working with senior staff). It is sometimes said that the most important decision of the board is to appoint the right person as CEO (or, in the case of a local church, as church leader). But this does not minimize the role of the board at all times.

## PRINCIPLES

The board ensures that the *principles* of the organization, especially in terms of its 'objects', are followed correctly. It also ensures that the CEO maintains the principles and the objectives (or purpose) of the organization, which do not change.

## POLICY

Matters of *policy* require careful discussion and are not changed lightly. Changes of policy would normally be agreed by the board. Depending on the matter in question, it may be helpful for the CEO and senior staff to draw in one or two board members for consultation as policy discussions progress.

## PRACTICE

Areas of *practice*, which must keep changing to retain effectiveness, will be delegated to the CEO as he/she works within the strategic direction set by the board.

# 2
# PROFILE OF AN EFFECTIVE BOARD
☑

An effective board for any spiritual enterprise will include members with specialist backgrounds, as outlined on pp21-25.[6] There are four essential marks common to all board members, namely:

(a) to be in full accord with the doctrinal basis of the movement / institution, and with its mission;

(b) to understand and endorse the need for this ministry in its wider context;

(c) to have (or work to build up) a grasp of the ministry's history and values;

(d) to demonstrate in their own lives a desire to grow in the knowledge and love of God.

As vacancies arise, the selection process for finding new board members may require wide consultation. This stage also gives opportunity to look at the make-up of the board. What is the gender balance like? The balance of ethnicity? Are there particular

---

6. As an expression of transparency, the names of board members should be easily accessible for anyone who would like to know. It can be useful to list them on your website, together with a brief bio, as well as in the *Annual Report*.

## THE ART OF GOOD GOVERNANCE

minorities who should be better represented?[7] Typically, a Nominations Committee is appointed by the board to search for candidates and propose them for final interview and election by the board. In some cases, especially in older charities, the election is conducted by a wider body of members, depending on the original Constitution.

In most charities, the board Chair is either elected from within the board by the existing board members, or directly appointed by the board after an external search. Either way, in the interests of stability, it is a good idea to agree from the start that, if possible, the Chair will serve for at least two successive terms.[8]

If board membership is limited to people the current board members already know, the ministry may be missing out on the best people. Often there can be a wrong assumption that the current leaders know all the best people. Some board members will be 'home-grown', that is, former staff of the mission agency or graduates of the student ministry, but each should be invited on the strength of the specialism or specific facets of wisdom and

> **THE MINISTRY MAY BE MISSING OUT ON THE BEST PEOPLE**

---

7. It is always good to be aware of the make-up of the board, to ensure that it appropriately reflects the life of the ministry, and for its greater effectiveness. In extending an invitation to new board members, it may be helpful to be clear that the invitation is to share in overseeing the *whole* ministry, and not to represent a particular group within that.

8. With each term lasting three or four years.

experience he or she brings. Every board needs at least one member with financial competence. That member is often given the role of board Treasurer. Where an additional board position can be filled by someone who also has a good understanding of financial matters, this is to be welcomed.

**FACETS OF WISDOM AND EXPERIENCE**
For bodies claiming charitable status, an increasing raft of policies and protocols is required by governments. Some will require an understanding of employment law, and of how to make a case for exemption on confessional grounds, where that is appropriate / possible. These cover, for example, policies on workplace safety; the safeguarding of children and vulnerable adults; the proper handling of donations; giving to external bodies; and the employment of people with protected characteristics. (See the Equality requirements in your country.)

Each of the following four facets is important in governing a ministry, to ensure the ministry's effectiveness, and to meet fiduciary responsibilities and associated legal accountability of the board:

(a) **a level of theological understanding** as is consonant with the objectives of the charity / ministry;

(b) **a grasp of current trends** in the area in which the movement or ministry is engaged, and a knowledge of trends in society as they relate to the mission of the movement. This pairing of trends (in ministry/society) will encompass sociological and philosophical trends, as well as theological and missiological trends;

(c) **deep experience in financial matters** and fund development; and an understanding of how to identify and manage the risks to which the ministry is exposed and to which its operations are susceptible. A clear understanding of financial matters is vital for financial planning. This does not require a major donor to be placed on a board because of that person's means.[9] All members, regardless of personal means, must be selected on the strength of their skills and experience, and their grasp of the mission or ministry;

(d) **familiarity with employment law**. This does not require having a board member who is professionally qualified in this area. But the board and CEO should identify a qualified person whom the CEO or HR manager could consult informally for advice and support, or formally for paid advocacy, if needed. In a ministry context, HR issues can require not only technical knowledge, but spiritual wisdom.

---

9. Some missions and charities have used Chris Wright and John Stott: *Money and the Gospel* (Dictum, 2019) in approaching donors. Part I covers Christian giving (for major donors, and for personal givers). Part ll covers the Apostle Paul's teaching on financial accountability. This will reassure donors that the organization is aware of the need for a careful accountability structure. It is the only such work of its kind, to our knowledge.

Related to this, it will be important for the CEO to ensure a clear grievance procedure is in place so staff know they will be listened to, and that they have recourse to an appeal process, in line with Matthew 18:15-18. This spiritual wisdom will avert much difficulty. However, these verses should not be applied woodenly and inappropriately. They do not refer to situations where an abuse of seniority or of power has been exercised. In such cases, a complainant may be unable to approach a senior colleague on his / her own; and in rare cases, outside authorities should be informed – for example, if illegal practice is suspected.[10]

> **ENSURE A CLEAR GRIEVANCE PROCEDURE IS IN PLACE**

Where a board has grown without careful strategy, it can be useful to have an audit of members' skills to identify any area of deep experience which is missing.[11] Then as members complete their term of service, their places can be taken by those

---

10. If illegal practice of any sort (and at any level) is suspected, the staff member in question should be placed on immediate leave. Legal authorities need to be given access to systems and devices, and freedom to interview colleagues. If it is the CEO who is under investigation, the board Chair will put in place an interim leader; if it is another staff member, the CEO will work with HR to arrange cover for responsibilities. If a member of the board is suspected of illegal practice, he or she should stand down immediately, pending investigation. The onus is on the board to ensure as quick a resolution as is possible.

11. Terms are usually for three or four years, and the Constitution will often provide for service of only two terms in succession without a break, though the Chair, Secretary and Treasurer may not be subject to that. Retirement for all members is often set around the age of seventy or seventy-five. This ensures that a board has stability, while continually being refreshed.

with the needed skills or experience. If aspects of understanding are lacking, the ministry will be weakened or jeopardized.

There may be testing times when, together, the board will have to work to discern the way forward. Based on a sense of the ministry's history and values, and each of the above facets of wisdom and experience, the board will play the role of the 'men of Issachar': those who understood the times, and who knew what to do (see 1 Chronicles 12:32). Each new appointment to the board is important to get right. As names arise, they will be discussed by the whole board, and the CEO's comments sought, before a final decision is reached.

> **EACH NEW APPOINTMENT IS IMPORTANT TO GET RIGHT**

Approaches should not be made informally by a board member to 'sound a person out'. It can create embarrassment if the board decides not to invite the person, or it can make the board feel under pressure to do so. All approaches must come only on the authority of the board after open discussion. Some boards invite potential members first to become participant-observers in one or two meetings before they commit themselves.

No board is immune from becoming weakened, and the board Chair must remain vigilant. The Chair needs to be watchful for voices on the board and in senior management that are too dominant, at the expense of quieter voices being heard.

There have been sad stories of boards which have lacked in one or more of those four facets of wisdom and experience, above, or have sat loose to their history or values, or have been over-zealous in drawing in younger and therefore inexperienced members.

On younger leaders: There are no rules, but having one or two board members under 35 seems good practice. Some agencies have an ongoing strategy of inviting younger people onto regional councils or special interest committees, and in this way younger people build their knowledge and skills, while being kept close to the hub.

> *HAVING ONE OR TWO BOARD MEMBERS UNDER 35 SEEMS GOOD PRACTICE*

A strategy to invest in able, committed, younger people, who learn the values and culture of the movement, will provide a rich pool of potential future board members, advisers, and volunteers, who will be invaluable for the ministry in a range of ways for decades to come.[12]

---

12. While the work of nurturing younger leaders will come under the CEO, the board will want to be kept briefed, as it is a vital aspect of the ministry's life. Board members past and present may be called upon to assist as 'older friends' to younger leaders.

# 3
# ORIENTATION OF NEW BOARD MEMBERS
☑

New members can familiarize themselves with recent Minutes, but that is not sufficient orientation. While board members each bring different specialisms, all need to become conversant with the past history of the movement, and the reason for its values. Only with this combination of history and values can a board calibrate ideas.

*HISTORY AND VALUES ENABLE A BOARD TO CALIBRATE IDEAS*

Together with the senior leaders, they can then work towards a future vision which is kept aligned with the original vision and purpose.

The nature of this orientation will depend on a range of factors. If new members come from outside, it could be good for them to be furnished with back copies of the Annual Report, or major items from regular news organs. This will help them build their grasp of history and values. If they live locally, they could be invited to lunch, to see the office and meet staff. Board members are worth time investment, while respect should be paid to their time and their other pressures.

# 4
# GUARDING THEOLOGICAL INTEGRITY AND FINANCIAL INTEGRITY

Formal structures need to be established to guard the theological integrity and the financial integrity of any ministry.

**THEOLOGICAL INTEGRITY**
The board may appoint a theological adviser, or theological working group, to be chaired by a board member. A small ministry may approach a larger trusted ministry to ask if their theological advisers may be willing to suggest names of people who would help in this capacity. If well-intentioned initiatives are introduced without deep biblical reflection, a movement could veer gradually and imperceptibly off-course. The theological integrity of an organization – whether a ministry or publishing house – will be maintained only with constant vigilance. This underlines the place of the doctrinal basis as an *anchor*. To change the metaphor, it also acts as a *flag* around which staff and supporters rally.

# THE ART OF GOOD GOVERNANCE

Some ministries have recognized the benefit of taking time to work through the doctrinal basis with all levels of leadership, from board to small groups, to ensure that both its tenets, and its dual roles of *anchor* and *flag*, are owned and understood. People can change their beliefs as years pass, and the invitation to signify continuing adherence to a doctrinal statement can be a good regular exercise for a board and for staff. Board and ministry staff of many bodies signify their adherence to the doctrinal basis each year by signing it. This should be no mere administrative exercise and the way the occasions are led by the Chair/CEO will set the tone.

## FINANCIAL INTEGRITY

Financial integrity extends to donor recruitment and development,[13] to all budgeting for ministry expenditure, staff salaries and pensions, and to investment and accounting.[14] These matters could be handled by a finance/business advisory group chaired, for example, by the Treasurer on behalf of the board. The CEO would normally be a member of this group. The Treasurer would then bring proposals to the board. This group's remit should include:

---

13. Donor letters and appeals should carry the right 'voice', whether coming from the CEO or from the Communications team. Does the writer reflect a reliance on God to prompt the giving, rather than putting pressure on potential givers? Does the letter set out clearly how money will be used, without inflating statistics? The values of the ministry are seen in the appeal letter as they are seen nowhere else.

14. See *Money and the Gospel* for biblical insight.

(a) understanding the provenance of all donations and other income, and whether such gifts and income are given with any restrictions or 'strings attached'. While rare, the question should also be asked as to whether there could be reputational damage in accepting a gift;

(b) ensuring that appropriate internal controls are in place within the ministry (including oversight of discretionary funds[15] and segregation of duties) to ensure that cash and other assets are protected from risks such as theft, fraud and unauthorized expenditure.

The board's responsibility in accepting a budget is based on its understanding of the figures presented. Some board members who are less familiar with accounts may need more explanation so they can participate in the discussion. The board as a whole will bring insight and foresight. It is critical for the board to be fully informed on financial matters, and for no information to be withheld. Lack of information can lead to uninformed judgment and cause irretrievable harm to a ministry. Accounts must be audited in compliance with Charity law. In some

> *THE BOARD AS A WHOLE WILL BRING INSIGHT AND FORESIGHT*

---

15. For a CEO or Chair to have a discretionary fund is now less common than it used to be. If such a fund is in place, the money should be fully accounted and audited just like all other funds, and should be used for purposes consonant with the objects of the ministry, rather than for wider charitable purposes.

situations, the recommendations of an auditor can usefully be shared with the wider support base, to alert them to important financial developments.

# 5
# THE CEO'S ROLE IN RELATION TO THE MINISTRY, AND TO THE BOARD
☑

The CEO is responsible for keeping the sights of his whole team set on the mission and purpose of the ministry. This is part of his overall management, which must remain 'aspirational' and not just functional.[16] A vital aspect of the role is to recruit and appoint senior staff.

Checks and balances are important. Many organizations have a rule that the appointments of all leaders of departments or functions will be confirmed by the board. While board members with particular interests or specialisms may be drawn into the interview process for senior appointments in an advisory capacity, it is good for the CEO to make the final decision, seeking the board's formal confirmation.

The CEO will work closely with the board Chair, who will often become the CEO's first-line confidant(e).

---

16. The tone set by the CEO will filter down through departments. There is much to stimulate thought and discussion on leadership with senior teams in a modern classic, *The Leadership Files: From around the world, across a century*. (Ajith Fernando, Vaughan Roberts et al. Dictum, 2021).

## THE ART OF GOOD GOVERNANCE

It is vital that a board Chair have capacity and ready availability for this commitment – and that each have a high level of trust in, and respect for, the other.

It is good practice for the CEO to be entitled to attend each of the board's sub-committees or working groups.

The CEO will often act as Secretary to the board. Board members need to be well-informed, with regular reports, and well-prepared papers for meetings, including a clear set of accounts. Accompanying papers will give board members the information they need to prepare for the meeting: judgments are only ever as good as the information on which they are based.[17] Ideally, Minutes of all meetings, once agreed for distribution by the Chair, should be sent out within two weeks at most, to ensure timely action on matters while the meeting is still fresh in people's minds. The Minutes will be amended, if necessary, and then agreed formally, in the following meeting.

### REPORTING AND APPRAISAL OF THE CEO

The CEO will report to the board through its Chair. The Chair will ensure that the CEO is appraised at least on an annual basis, often with a less formal mid-year review / conversation but this should not become a

---

17. Each accompanying paper should bear (above the title) the date of the meeting and the number of the Agenda item to which it refers. It should also bear the name of the writer, which may be the CEO, a head of function, board member, or an invited party. Papers should be distributed early enough to give board members time to consider their contents carefully.

burden in terms of extra reports required. There is no single pattern for formal appraisal. Sometimes in larger organizations, three or four board members, including the Chair, would meet with the CEO for an unhurried session, and work through major strands of the ministry: their current shape/state; their challenges; and the CEO's leadership of them, personally and through the senior team.

The board appraisal should not be seen as threatening, but as an expression of partnership. It is a means of confirming that a) the board and the staff continue to share a common vision; and b) the CEO is proving effective as a leader. It also provides an opportunity to ensure that the CEO is adequately provided for, and a chance to address any other issues of wellbeing – including that of family members.[18]

> **THE BOARD APPRAISAL SHOULD NOT BE SEEN AS THREATENING**

If the relationship between the CEO and the board Chair is good, the board Chair will naturally be enquiring about the CEO's health and ministry more frequently, as well as about the morale of the team. If anything seems awry, there will then be an opportunity to explore that in the context of friendly trust.

---

18. Informal accountability is also significant. Leaders and Trustees who are spiritually healthy will have informal structures in church life and in friendships which will be of significance. A desire for Christian fellowship will issue naturally from personal discipleship. If a leader/Trustee (or their family) gradually move to the periphery of church life, it could be a sign that not all is well, and a gentle enquiry by a trusted friend, or by a church leader, could be timely, and welcomed.

# THE ART OF GOOD GOVERNANCE

**THE BOARD AND THE STAFF TEAM**

Opportunities for the whole board and the senior team to meet each other can strengthen a sense of trust and partnership. Such gatherings will also help the board to understand more of the ministry dynamics, and any strains, and to know of pressures felt.

In addition to meeting senior staff, it can be good for board members to meet staff at all levels, if there is opportunity, to offer encouragement, to keep their finger on the pulse, and to get a feel for the culture of the organization on the ground. In conversation with staff, board members must be mindful that the board operates only as a whole body, and individual members should avoid giving any wrong impression that they speak for the board, or carry any personal authority. Board authority is exercised only in meetings which are quorate, and where members vote on issues, on the strength of informed discussion.

It is good practice to invite leaders of ministries / functions to be present at board meetings where the board will discuss matters which relate to their area, so they and the board can hear each other's insights.

## APPOINTMENT OF A NEW CEO

A good board will always have succession in the back of its members' minds. The new leader must embody the values of the organization, and want its vision to develop in line with its history and its principles. There is a needed humility for a new leader in this way. (An entrepreneurial starter of new ventures, a wonderful gift for other contexts, is unlikely to be a good fit.) Some potential new CEOs have been identified well in advance, and trained up for succession. Or they may be former younger leaders (see p25) or former committee members, now in other roles; or they may come from outside. Whatever the route, the new leader will want to build on the work of the current leader.

The board will typically determine the job description and profile for the CEO, then the Nominations Committee will start to receive suggestions of names, and to search for candidates who a) fit the profile; and b) demonstrate the necessary experience. As with the appointing of new board members, work will be needed to ensure that the best person is found, as he or she may not already be known to the board. To reach this stage, some boards will employ a trusted search agency. From the search, the Nominations Committee, in consultation with the board Chair, will ideally nominate two or three candidates for an interview process.

It is unwise for the board Chair and the CEO of a charity or ministry to be members of the same family. Greater accountability is required than this relationship could afford. Should the board appoint a CEO who is a close friend of the Chair, a wise Chair will stand down and hand over his/her office.

> **IT IS UNWISE FOR THE CHAIR AND CEO TO BE FAMILY MEMBERS, OR CLOSE FRIENDS**

A close friendship in this context, even with the best of intentions on both sides, could impede objective appraisal of the CEO and his/her leadership. Further, this would leave the staff feeling vulnerable, as they would now not be able to appeal past their CEO with any confidence, if the need were to arise. And as a corollary, when a change of Chair is needed, it would be wise for a board not to appoint as its Chair a close friend of the serving CEO. While it is a rare and serious step to have to appeal past a CEO, such a course of action may become necessary as a last resort, and provision needs to be there for it.

The chosen candidate will demonstrate proven ability in the following: a) to work under authority; b) to delegate confidently; and c) to work with staff who have greater gifts in some areas.

Each of these abilities can be explored in interview. The new CEO must be able to lead with confidence, under the authority of the board.[19] The board's direction and setting of strategy is a means of enabling a CEO, not a means of policing. The interviewing procedure should probe past experience and consider how a person dealt with real situations in previous roles. 'What would you do if...' questions are to be avoided. Instead ask: 'Tell us of a time when... What did you do?' The old adage is worth remembering – that the best predictor of future behaviour is past behaviour.

> **THE INTERVIEW SHOULD PROBE PAST EXPERIENCE**

There is no 'pass' or 'fail' in the appointment procedure. We believe that the Lord creates the good works for us to do. While most new CEOs will meet a majority of the prescribed skills and abilities, any remaining gaps can usually be filled either by further training or by redistribution / delegation of tasks. In any case, at the interview stage there is always an option not to appoint any of the candidates, and to extend the search process. Psychometric testing may be worth considering as part of a second interview for senior staff, or for the selection of new board members. It can confirm strengths and weaknesses while potentially highlighting an area which conventional interviewing could miss.

---

19. That is, understanding the partnership between them in pursuing the goals of the organization / movement, focusing on its priorities, and avoiding 'mission creep'.

# 6
# BOARD PROTOCOL
☑

Board Chairs of Christian ministries are likely to include a brief devotion at the beginning of a meeting, or prayer at the end. In terms of the board business, the following protocols are generally observed.

**HANDLING MAJOR ISSUES**
Board decisions, by their nature, will have long-term impact and should not be rushed. Major issues can be brought to the board (with supporting papers) for preliminary discussion, with a view to more discussion at the following meeting, before a vote is taken. It may require further thought, prayer, consultation, and fact-finding before a decision can be reached.[20] Discussion in meetings is best handled through the Chair at all times, and conflicting views can then be heard, calibrated, and where necessary, mediated.

---

20. If a vote is unanimous, it should be recorded by using that word. The Latin *nem con* is ambiguous. Its meaning is 'no-one against', and that can include instances where some members abstained. The word 'unanimous' is unambiguous. A major decision with a unanimous vote gives a clear message to the wider body, and, in future years, to those researching aspects of a movement's history. Abstentions are vital to note for a true record.

## CYCLE OF BUSINESS

The board Secretary will ensure an annual cycle of business, so all aspects of the calendar year are overseen. Each meeting should include at least one substantial discussion, an item which gives the board 'something to bite on'. The Chair and Secretary can work to facilitate a periodic self-review of the board in terms of its effective leadership and its development. This review can sometimes take the form of a residential overnight meeting.

## CONFLICTS OF INTEREST

It is good practice for all Trustees to declare all conflicts of interest annually; these can then be assessed for their materiality and any appropriate action taken, should problems be envisaged. In addition, conflicts of interest for any agenda item need to be declared at the start of the meeting. These conflicts may be obvious, or more nuanced.[21]

## DEPENDENT COMMITTEES

Such groups often include specialists in the field or appropriate senior staff. The board should agree Terms of Reference for its sub-committees.[22]

---

21. For example, *pro bono* work from board members' friends is to be welcomed, but care must be taken that this not be rewarded in less-tangible ways, such as using the charity's name to seek further voluntary sector clients.

22. Terms of Reference should cover the role and scope of the group, frequency of reporting, and, if set up for a time-critical purpose, the envisaged length of the group's service. T of R could also include the distribution list of Agendas and Minutes. (These sometimes go out more widely, as a means of ongoing consultation, and of informing.)

# 7
# SUPPORTING THE BOARD
☑

The Secretary will work closely with the Chair in preparing Agendas and Minutes for board meetings. The Agenda will ideally be sent out at least two weeks in advance to allow time for board members to read all papers unhurriedly, and pray. If there are major issues they wish to raise at the meeting, this also gives a chance for them to contact the Chair or Secretary in advance, to alert them.

The Secretary will be responsible for agreeing the Minutes with the Chair before they are sent out, and then for tracking the action points to ensure each is addressed. Careful Minutes are vital, not only as a means for tracking action points, but also in creating the historical archive of the ministry. Further, they will inform future discussions, so the movement can learn from its history. For clarity in the historical record, it is best practice for members to be referred to with a full Christian name or more than one initial, rather than a single initial: Peter or Petra Smith or P Y Smith, rather than simply P Smith.

> **CAREFUL MINUTES WILL INFORM FUTURE DISCUSSIONS**

## SEVEN RULES

If a member arrives late to a meeting or leaves a meeting early, that should be recorded in the list of those present, after his or her name (eg <Item 7 onwards> or <Items 1-8> etc). This is important, especially where a major issue has been discussed, to avoid lack of clarity about who participated in the discussion and the vote.

Physical sets of Minutes should be indexed, and bound every five years, together with appropriate accompanying papers. Archive libraries will require such physical copies for future historians, alongside a digital archive, transferred as needed over time to successive new forms of storage.

◆ ◆ ◆

# TO CONCLUDE

So we come to a close. Seven liberating rules which, when staked into the ground, will free you up to focus on the *mission* of the organization. These rules are gold, and it may be useful to re-read them every year or two. As we've seen, there is no eighth rule, but no ministry or charity will survive on six.

Contexts vary, and adjustments may be needed. While written for a ministry context, there are, as noted, transferable principles for secular charities.

*SPIRITUAL WISDOM IS ALWAYS PRACTICAL WISDOM*

Spiritual wisdom is always practical wisdom.

We land back where we started on the message of 1 Corinthians 4:2. Staying aligned to the original purpose and 'objects' will require constant vigilance. If you give that vigilance, you will prove faithful.

◆ ◆ ◆

*'Clarity and brevity are two great gifts to the world.'*

Dictum, based in Oxford, UK, was founded in 2018. We publish books of global worth (biography, history, doctrine, mission, Christian life). Our list includes classic reprints.

For movements, agencies or churches wishing to purchase any title in bulk, we will, if required, include your logo and a description of your ministry at the front of the books purchased.

As part of our ministry, we make available at no cost a small library of 14 ebooks in any country where the church has fewer resources, and to students globally. *The Art of Good Governance* is in this collection. See our website for more.

Our titles are available on all the usual platforms. Online bookstores are found in the UK at *churchbooks.co.uk* and in the US at *goodread.store*.

Review copies are available at no charge. Please use the contact form on our website.

*dictumpress.com*

**books worth reading more than once**

This could not have come at a more timely moment. Full of practical advice – an excellent refresher for experienced board members and Chairs, and indispensable when it comes to recruiting and inducting new board members and senior executives. I wholeheartedly recommend it.

**Ram Gidoomal CBE** *Former Chair: Stewardship Services; Former Chair: Lausanne Movement*

Good governance is a key to fruitful, sustainable, resilient ministry. These foundational principles and practices will help you grasp your responsibilities, and successfully navigate the complexities you will inevitably encounter.

**Tim Adams** *General Secretary, IFES (International Fellowship of Evangelical Students)*

Accountability is a godly principle and an essential aspect of good governance. This guide brings clarity to the complementary roles of the board and CEO, and to board make-up, skills and responsibilities.

**Nola Leach** *Co-leader: European Leadership Forum Politics and Society Network; Former CEO, CARE*

Many charities have floundered for want of a good board that knows its role. This excellent and practical guidance will benefit both novice and experienced board members.

**Allan Beckett** *Director and Founder, Carnelian*

- ☑ Board members of organizations, seminaries, publishing houses
- ☑ Chief Executive Officers and their senior leadership teams
- ☑ Transferable principles for school heads and governors, and for church leaders and councils